An ama Management Briefing

Worker Volunteering: A New Resource for the 1980s

Kerry Kenn Allen

A Division of American Management Associations

Library of Congress Cataloging in Publication Data

Allen, Kerry Kenn.
  Worker volunteering.

  (An AMA management briefing)
    1. Industry—Social aspects—United States.
  2. Volunteer workers in social service—United States.
  3. Voluntarism—United States.   I. Title. II. Series:
  American Management Associations.   AMA management
  briefing.
  HD60.5.U5A44   361.7'65'0973   80-14959
  ISBN 0-8144-2245-4 (pbk.)

*This Management Briefing has been distributed to all mem-
bers enrolled in the Human Resources Division of the
American Management Associations. A limited supply of
extra copies is available at $5.00 a copy for AMA members,
$7.50 for nonmembers.*

First Printing

Contents

About the Author

Kerry Kenn Allen is executive vice president of VOLUNTEER: The National Center for Citizen Involvement, created as a result of the June 1979 merger of the National Center for Voluntary Action (NCVA) and the National Information Center on Volunteerism. Previously, he had served as the NCVA's executive director and chief operating officer and held several other administrative positions. A consultant for numerous voluntary organizations, he gained his early experience through administrative work at the University of Illinois at Urbana-Champaign where he received a B.A. and completed course work for an M.A. in higher education. His many publications include: *Volunteers from the Workplace* and *The Wichita Experience: Mobilizing Corporate Resources to Meet Community Needs*. He has also contributed to the magazine, *Voluntary Action Leadership*.

Introduction

THE 1970s were termed the "Me Decade" by social observers, reflecting the self-centered orientation and concern of people for themselves. Paradoxically, the same decade saw an unprecedented growth in the interest of people to help others in need.

Today, millions of Americans volunteer their time, talent, efforts, and energy to help solve the social problems which had once been left to the government to deal with. An estimated 37 million people—roughly one out of every four Americans over the age of 14—are now engaged in volunteer activities in their communities. The value of organized volunteer service was estimated in 1976 to be over $30 billion a year. If unorganized services were included, that total would be doubled. The fact is that volunteers have become an essential part of the solution to this country's problems.

Volunteers get a deep satisfaction in helping solve pressing human, social, and environmental problems. In doing so, they help improve the quality of life, and they control those divisions that affect their lives and the lives of their neighbors. A 1978 Gallup Poll concluded that 89 percent of the citizens in urban areas would be willing, if asked, to participate in a volunteer service activity. The total time willing to be committed was over one billion hours per month.

Most of the material for this briefing is drawn from the Volunteers from the Workplace project conducted by the National Center for Voluntary Action (NCVA) in 1978-79 (see Appendix).

Citations of specific company programs are based on the companies' responses to a written survey and to telephone and personal interviews. An expansion of this information can be found in NCVA's book, *Volunteers from the Workplace*, published in 1979. This briefing is drawn from the research done by several members of the NCVA staff—Shirley Keller, Isolde Chapin, Donna Hill, and Feroza Allee—and reflects a vast body of information accumulated over 15 months of research and analysis.

1

An Overview of the Employee Volunteer Movement

EMPLOYEE volunteer programs are still in their infancy. Most of them are barely two or three years old. In terms of their relative development, they are approximately at the point where college volunteer programs were ten years ago or where hospital volunteer programs were 20 years ago. They are only beginning to develop the sophistication of other forms of volunteering.

Basically, there are five types of employee volunteer programs: individual matching, group projects, released time, loaned personnel, and social service leave.

Individual matching. Some corporations create structures to match individual employees with specific jobs that need to be done.

Group projects. The most visible of all corporate-based volunteering, group projects are a way to focus on specific, often short-term, projects. They also offer a nonthreatening way for employees to volunteer, since volunteers work with their colleagues and friends. Group projects are relatively economical and lend themselves easily to control by the employees involved.

Released time. Simply put, released time is giving employees time off with pay to volunteer for community service activities.

Loaned personnel. A natural extension of released time is to loan personnel to community agencies to undertake specific projects for a period of time, ranging from a week to several months. An employee may be used to supplement existing staff on a project—for example, to help with a fund-raising campaign or perhaps to improve the management of the host agency. Originally, such programs were open only to executives, but they are now open to all employees in many companies.

Social service leave. This relatively new program relieves employees from their job responsibilities for up to a year. They may be paid full salary and benefits and are guaranteed comparable employment on their return. Employees on social service leave are free to focus on their community-based assignment.

The National Center for Voluntary Action (NCVA) not long ago carried out a survey of major U.S. corporations regarding their programs and policies for helping community groups (see Appendix). In all, 364 companies responded to the survey, representing a 10 percent return. Of these, 333 companies reported they had some form of employee volunteer program. Below are the different ways in which companies provided help, together with the number of responding companies giving such help.

Activities	*Number of companies*
Donated materials or services	289
Loaned personnel	262
Released time	239
Gave recognition to employees who volunteer	229
Provided executives on boards	220
Sponsored group projects	207
Provided a clearinghouse within company	126
Donated grants or contributions through employees	125
Allowed recruitment on company premises	53
Offered social service leave	40

The survey also revealed, however, that for the most part, employee volunteer programs are still not taken seriously. They are given low priority and are not being given the necessary resources to be successful.

Only 6 percent of the companies responding had full-time staff assigned to the volunteer programs. Virtually no company kept records on the number of employees who volunteer or the amount of time contributed. In fact companies with released time programs generally had little idea of how much these programs actually cost the company. Surprisingly, few companies had well-articulated goals for their programs and even fewer could describe the criteria by which they could be evaluated.

INGREDIENTS FOR SUCCESS

Despite their relative youth, corporate programs have begun to display specific characteristics that indicate whether they will be successful. The NCVA has identified five main ingredients for success:

- The corporation must be committed to the program, provide the necessary resources, and treat the program in the same way it would any other business undertaking.
- The chief executive must take a personal interest in the program and make this interest known throughout the company.
- The program must have an atmosphere of legitimacy that constantly reinforces the employees' interest.
- The program must have sound management, with articulated goals, policies, and procedures.
- Good working relationships must be created and maintained with the community.

The best volunteer programs tend to be those that are concerned with employee welfare generally and that provide many creative opportunities for the personal development of individual employees.

2

The Different Types of Company Programs

NO two communities are alike. The geography, the industries, and the people of each combine in a unique way. Similarly, no two companies are alike. They may be in the same city or may even occupy the same building; but the way in which they approach their work, their environment, their interest in the larger community—all of these will differ.

There is no standard approach to employee volunteering. Each company must discover the way in which it can best mobilize its resources within the context of its own interests and internal demands. A few corporations operate all the major program models, committing full-time staff to program management. Most others offer the one or two models that fit their situation. The important thing is that corporations are beginning to seek ways they can better serve their employees and their communities through volunteering.

RECRUITMENT AND MATCHING INDIVIDUAL INTERESTS

At the heart of every volunteer activity is the willingness of a single individual to become involved in solving a problem or filling a need. Whether it be through a one-to-one relationship or through participation in a group service project, individual action is the point at which volunteering actually takes place.

Much of the work of volunteer administrators deals with matching individuals with specific jobs that need to be done. Corporations have found that such matching efforts are an excellent way to begin employee volunteer programs. Matching has the advantage of appealing to a large number of employees, since at least in theory, everyone can find something of interest. It can also be a relatively economical approach to employee involvement, not necessarily requiring a large commitment of staff time.

Perhaps the most elementary matching method is to invite an agency like the local Voluntary Action Center (VAC) to come to the company and recruit. The company may pave the way for the VAC by running announcements in the in-house employee publication, posting notices in public places, or otherwise informing employees of the opportunity to volunteer.

Over 300 VACs are affiliated with the National Center for Voluntary Action, and they recruit over 250,000 volunteers annually and refer them to some 36,000 agencies. The VACs make every effort to meet the volunteer's needs—timing, interests, logistics—at the same time responding to the specific needs identified by the agencies they serve. Not only is the VAC concerned with the quantity of volunteer service, it is also concerned with the quality of that service.

In Washington, D.C., the Chesapeake and Potomac Telephone Company relies on the VAC to do the volunteer placement. The company has 120 worksites within the District of Columbia alone. Employees who are interested in volunteering fill out forms that are sent to the VAC which in turn conducts the interviews and makes the placements. The company's volunteer coordinator then assumes responsibility for follow-up with the volunteers to insure their satisfaction with the placement.

Some companies actually commit full-time staff resources to matching efforts. At Bell Laboratories in Murray Hill, N.J., for example, Belle Thompson maintains an extensive file of volunteer opportunities in the community, spends the needed time in screening and follow-up, and reduces the time lag between the expression of interest by the volunteer and the actual placement. As a result, the company only loses about 10 percent of its volunteers every year, and most of these are people who leave the area.

At Shell Oil in Houston, a list of organizations and a list of sample jobs are developed and maintained by the volunteer coordinator, Pat Loman. The prospective volunteer reviews both lists. During the interview both the employee and the coordinator try to clarify the employee's interests and come up with at least two alternative placements. Agencies call to request volunteers, but Ms. Loman also seeks out new possibilities on her own.

In 1977, the National Center for Voluntary Action (NCVA) undertook a special one-year project designed to create and test a new model for recruiting corporate workers, with special focus on those in nonmanagement positions who had not before been involved in a volunteer job. The project involved 14 cooperating corporations in Wichita, Kan., and the local VAC. The companies were asked to identify one person who would be allowed up to five hours per week of released time to serve as the in-plant coordinator (IPC). His or her job was to receive from the VAC descriptions of volunteer jobs in the community. While the IPC was encouraged to use all available communications channels within the company, the emphasis was on direct, one-to-one communication with other employees. This peer recruitment model resulted in over 400 new volunteers in less than six month's time. More importantly, it demonstrated that a corporation, working in partnership with a local VAC, could make a significant contribution of employee volunteers from a relatively small investment of its resources.

The NVAC's Wichita Project illustrated that the key to a successful matching program is the partnership that is established with community agencies. The in-house recruitment and referral services are only as good as the information on which they are based. If job descriptions are complete, if the agency is willing to adequately orient and supervise volunteers, if the agency is prepared to adjust to the employees' needs, the match can be successfully made.

GROUP PROJECTS

Group projects focus both human and financial resources on specific projects. They also have the potential of involving all employees, from the chief executive and senior executives to clerks and secretaries. Often the only prerequisite for participation is a willingness to work. In a fund-raising walkathon, a playground repair project, or a Christmas party, volunteers do not need to worry about specific skills and expertise. What is more important is their energy, commitment, and interest.

Employees are often delighted to work as part of a team, free from competitive pressures, in an atmosphere conducive to mixing with co-workers and making new friends. Most projects turn out to be more fun than work with volunteers discovering enjoyment in joining with others in helping activities.

Group projects are also a highly flexible way for companies to undertake employee involvement programs. While some companies, such as Levi Strauss, have developed sophisticated community involvement teams, many more give the primary responsibility to a volunteer coordinator. Still more companies simply respond to requests from the community through existing company structures or through ad hoc employee groups. Once established, the system for handling group projects can become self-perpetuating, requiring little administrative oversight.

Group projects are usually directed toward a single limited goal. For example, H. B.Fuller employees in Minneapolis, Minn., planted $8,000 worth of trees in four different locations around the city. A group of New York Telephone employees in the South Bronx section of the city spent a summer helping the Parks Department clean a large park. Employees of Union Oil in Schaumburg, Ill., participated in a variety show along with other entertainers to raise funds for a school's music department.

Ongoing projects may be extensions of one-shot efforts, or they may be focused around a need that must be addressed on a continuing basis. For example, at U.S. National Bank of Oregon in Portland, employees are involved in Project HOPE (Homebound Opportunities for Programming Education), an ongoing project which trains severely handicapped individuals to program computers in their homes. EDP programmers are given two or three hours per week released time to go out and teach the participants. At the end of the instruction, students are able to work on a contractual basis as programmers working from their homes. Some work for the bank itself part-time.

Many corporations encourage their employees to work in youth projects, with the most popular being Junior Achievement. JA is a nonprofit national organization established to introduce high school students to the principles and values of the free enterprise system. Under the guidance of volunteer advisors from corporations, students can learn the ins and outs of running a small business.

John Thomas, president of Chevron Research, part of Standard Oil of California, recently spent a year working with Junior Achievement. "The program has two values," he said, "educating youngsters about our economic system's success and more importantly, giving young people a sense of achievement and accomplishment. [It] is instrumental in getting them interested in learning while in school and interested in getting a job."

A number of companies also assist in educational projects, some going so far as to "adopt-a-school," establishing a continuing relationship through which the company responds to a laundry list of needs. New England Mutual Insurance in Boston adopted a high school, providing tutors, advisors for student interns and speakers on career opportunities.

The Northrop Corporation in Hawthorne, Ca., brings high school students into company offices to learn what it takes to do various jobs. The High School Involvement Program (HIP) involves students two hours a day, five days a week for 16 weeks. Participants receive credit equivalent to two classes.

Levi Strauss' Community Involvement Teams are one of the most organized approaches to group projects. The teams, established with the assistance of the company's Community Affairs Department, exist in over 60 locations. Once created, the groups are coordinated and managed by the employees, with the Community Affairs staff available to provide technical assistance and support services. At each worksite, the team determines what projects will be undertaken, taking into account the needs of the community and the interests and resources of the workers. Decisions are made by the employees, not the company. Management is encouraged to participate in the program without taking it over. As a result, Strauss employees have become active in a variety of projects:

- In El Paso, they raised more than $10,000 for a camp for disadvantaged children, then dug post holes and helped prepare the new camp site;

- In Ramer, Tenn., they planted four acres of soybeans and used profits from selling the crop to finance a new community park;
- In Winston-Salem, they escorted senior citizens around the Dixie Classic Fair;
- In Wichita Falls, they volunteered their time to paint and to assemble cribs for a day-care center.

Most group projects will never bring great change to a community; they are not usually designed to do so. Rather, they are a way for employees to reach out to others in need and to engage in the kind of activities that otherwise would go undone. The only real limit to these projects is the imagination of the volunteers and of the leaders of the agencies with which they work.

RELEASED TIME

Released time is both a model and a mechanism.

As a model, it is a way of recognizing employees' interest in volunteering and of encouraging and rewarding that interest. In most cases, the corporation is not sponsoring or managing a particular activity. Rather, it is offering the opportunity for employees to pursue their community interests on company time.

As a mechanism, it may be an appropriate supplement to company efforts to match employees to specific volunteer jobs or to sponsor group projects. In this case, released time offers an opportunity for the company itself to volunteer by absorbing the cost of wages as part of its total responsibility to the community. Although purists may argue whether employees who serve during company time are truly volunteers, supporters of released time point to the benefits of the practice and to the ways in which it facilitates employees' involvement.

At General Telephone of Florida, all employees are offered released time, and the company publishes a booklet listing community agencies and the volunteer assignments they have available. Employees are free to select the agency which interests them and to request the time off that may be necessary to fill the specific job.

Employees of E.B. Industries in Simsbury, Conn., provide much of the emergency fire and ambulance services for the community on a regular schedule of released time. In East Aurora, N.Y., employees of Fisher-Price Toys do much the same thing: two employees at a time are always available to respond to emergency calls.

Employees of Allstate Insurance in Jackson, Miss., and of Honeywell in New York City are among many who take part in telephone reassurance programs in which volunteers phone the handicapped and the elderly daily to ease their loneliness, to identify their needs, and to offer contact with the outside world.

The benefits that accrue to the community from such released time activities are clear. Agencies gain human resources during the daytime hours when demand may be greatest. (For some places— such as schools, clinics, and very small agencies—volunteers are only of value during the day.) In communities like Simsbury and East Aurora, for example, released time offers the best opportunity to answer an otherwise insoluble community problem.

But the company also benefits. In many cases, released time allows the company to target its resources, ensuring the greatest possible impact on the community. Also, like other employee volunteer activities, released time may improve relations between the corporation and the community. Finally, and perhaps most importantly, the company benefits from employees who are enthusiastic about their involvement as volunteers and are thus more committed to their jobs.

Edward J. Leitz, vice president for administration at Prudential Insurance Co. in Boston, summarized that benefit:

> ". . . the reasons we have released employees to serve as school volunteers have to do partly with our commitment to the city of Boston and its school system. However, from a selfish point of view, I feel that the amount of time spent by our employees in the school system, working with youngsters, allows our employees to broaden their awareness of their own environment; and we, as employers, are paid tenfold with individuals who are better balanced and more mature in their approach to both their job and the community in which they live."

Although released time programs demand a willingness on the part of the company to give actual, measurable resources to the community, most such programs are not formally structured and often escape the burden of stringent record-keeping and reporting. However, it is clear that three elements are critical to a successful released time program.

First, the program should operate within the framework of a stated policy. Such a policy statement is a clear indication to employees of the interest and commitment of the company. It ensures that all employees understand the program, and it may relieve the anxieties of middle managers and line supervisors. It also helps maintain the program over time.

Second, there must be operational guidelines which clearly delineate who may be involved and what the extent of their involvement can be. Many companies choose to limit released time to managers, believing that their time is more flexible. Managers are also better able to meet the overall demands of their jobs. Other companies limit the amount of released time any individual employee may use, and some companies require a match of one hour of personal time for every hour of released time.

Third, top management must support the program and middle managers must understand and accept the program. Without top management support, the program will founder and will be plagued by insecurity of both managers and employees. The support must be ongoing and visible and must reflect an awareness of the program's accomplishments.

In virtually every company, the decision about whether to set up a released time program is ultimately made not by the employee volunteer but by his or her supervisor. The realistic fears of these supervisors that they will be penalized for a drop in productivity because of their employees' community involvement must be understood and assuaged.

Enabling employees to volunteer during working hours need not reduce a corporation's productivity. Released time volunteers often make up missed work time and are often even more productive in their jobs because they do the same amount of work in fewer hours.

LOANED PERSONNEL

Perhaps the best known of all employee volunteer programs are those involving loaned personnel. Essentially, they are mechanisms

17

through which a corporation can make available to the community otherwise unavailable skills or expertise. Such loans predate released time volunteering or social service leave.

Although traditionally most companies loan out executives, these programs are being expanded to include all employees, particularly those who have specific professional skills. Thus, there are many examples of loaned personnel programs that have had a positive impact on the community.

For United Way of America, the practice of "borrowing" people began before World War II. Today, it is an integral part of United Way's total fund-raising campaign. Consistent with experiences others have had with employee volunteering, United Way emphasizes that loaning personnel benefits the company and the individual employee, not just United Way and the community. Indeed, in many communities, Loaned Executive Alumni Associations have been formed in direct response to the continuing interest of those who have served.

United Way, working cooperatively with the federal agency, ACTION, has most recently undertaken to demonstrate the value of loaned personnel in improving the management of nonprofit organizations. Based in Cincinnati, the Management Assistance Project matches professionally skilled employees with community agencies. Volunteers work in such areas as general management, personnel administration, goal setting, accounting, proposal development, determination of cost effectiveness, fiscal projections, and facility renovation. John Glaser, vice president of the Services Outreach Division of United Way sees the greatest benefit of the program as "exposing well-educated, middle-class corporate executives to the problems of the inner cities and poverty areas and, at the same time, increasing the awareness of the agencies to the corporate community." The personalizing of these relationships, Mr. Glaser believes, is an important measure of the program's strength.

The National Alliance of Business (NAB) relies on loaned personnel to sustain their efforts to address the problems of youth unemployment. Since the formation of NAB in 1968, more than 40,000 men and women have been on loan to the organization, some for up to two years. Their efforts have resulted in the securing of more than 3.5 million jobs, and the value of their contributed services has been estimated at over $20 million.

Since 1965, the Economic Development Council (EDC) of New York City, has helped businesses to help the city through the careful placement of loaned personnel throughout public agencies. EDC works closely, and only upon invitation, with city government officials to insure that the task being undertaken is important and that the loaned employee will have the tools available to make a positive contribution.

Even at the federal level, agencies make use of loaned personnel. The President's Reorganized Project, for example, has recruited 39 executives from 31 companies to assist in the effort to reorganize and improve the efficiency of government agencies.

In 1975, the Norton Company of Worcester, Mass., created its Loaned Executive Council—which actually works with all middle management and professional employees. Through the council, Norton coordinates loaned personnel from 20 local companies. While some projects may require only a single volunteer, others, like the preparation of the city budget, may require up to 20 participants. The company's fifth annual public report on social responsibility summarizes its approach to the project:

> "While personnel trained in business management techniques are not equipped to solve all the problems faced by communities, there are many ways businesses can help state and municipal governments. Loaning executives to work on those problems is a proven way for companies to improve the cities, and towns, where they are located. Normally, the community cannot afford to purchase the service or advice that businesses can provide."

Since 1971, IBM has provided loaned personnel who act as faculty members at minority colleges and universities. During the 1977-78 academic year, the company assisted 28 institutions in this way. Employees continue on full salary, and the company pays needed moving expenses. Participants are chosen from a pool of volunteers. Citibank also has a Loaned Executive and Professional Program that has been in operation for almost ten years. Most placements are in the New York metropolitan area.

Because of their long history, loaned personnel programs seem to operate more smoothly than other forms of employee volunteering. Some issues remain unsettled, however. For example, individuals in the programs fear that management does not view their work in the company as important. They worry that they have been let go too easily and that someone will take their place if they are away on community work for a week or a month. Such fears need to be brought out in the open—they may be real enough—if people on loan are to be effective.

SOCIAL SERVICE LEAVE

Social service leave programs are in many ways a step beyond other forms of employee volunteering. Pioneered by IBM, Xerox, and Wells Fargo Bank, leave programs enable employees to take extended periods of time, sometimes up to a year, away from their job, at either full or partial pay with a guarantee of continued equivalent employment upon their return. Although the company may ask the purpose of the leave, it is rare for an employee's request to be turned down because of the nature of the task to be undertaken.

Whereas social service leaves clearly include many of the self-renewal aspects of a sabbatical, they are focused on service to others—most often, service that is totally unrelated to the employee's job. Some examples of leaves approved by the three companies are:

- Working in a halfway house for alcoholics, developing workshops and materials to help re-integration into the community;
- Establishing a new chapter of Big Brothers;
- Initiating a nutritional program for elderly Mexican-Americans;
- Administering and evaluating psychological tests for the handicapped and helping with job placement;
- Providing counseling and career orientation for troubled youths; and
- Establishing a job training program for inner city minorities.

At IBM, social service leave is not viewed as a career-advancing experience. It is strictly something the employee volunteers want to do. There is no appraisal of performance while on leave: it is possible that employees on leave will learn things that will be useful on their jobs, but that is not necessarily so. Nor is it a requirement.

20

At IBM, Xerox, and Wells Fargo, social service leave is open to all employees, and the programs have attracted a variety of personnel from different levels. The Wells Fargo program, for example, has primarily involved persons from lower-level management and clerical jobs. Xerox's has attracted a wide mix of job levels, while IBM's has attracted primarily management employees.

Employees are relatively free to choose any project or to work with any agency, although typically the agencies must be non-profit, and engaged in social welfare, health, and related activities. Partisan political work is generally ruled out.

As with released time programs, the employees' immediate supervisor plays a role in the decision about social service leave. At IBM, for example, the manager is involved in the entire decision-making process and permission is implied when the application is forwarded for review. At both Xerox and Wells Fargo, employees wishing to take social service leave are not required to obtain their supervisor's permission, but in both companies, the supervisor does retain the right to appeal the approval or to ask that the leave be deferred temporarily.

Perhaps the most difficult aspect of social service leave is the return to the job at the end of the leave period. Policies are similar at each company. Wells Fargo and Xerox, for example, guarantee a return to the same job or to one at the same level and with the same future opportunity. At IBM, the employee's manager is seen as the key to successful re-entry: the manager who permits employees to go on leave is responsible for what happens on their return. Managers and employees keep in touch with each other during the course of the leave and make plans about the return so it is not left to the last minute. Staying in touch is also very important at Wells Fargo. Employees on leave must submit a report at the halfway point of their leave. Their supervisors also visit them once and call them every other week towards the close of the leave.

Certainly, social service leave is not a program that will be rapidly adopted by a great number of companies. It requires a serious commitment of company resources as well as a basic commitment to providing opportunities for employees to grow outside the company as well as within it. Only IBM, Xerox, and Wells Fargo have successfully undertaken social service leave programs on a major scale. But it is clear from their experiences that such programs do benefit the company and the employee as well as the community. It is this successful blend of results that has convinced them that social service leave is a valuable addition to their total community service program.

INVOLVING THE RETIRED WORKER

The inclusion of retirees in volunteer programs is natural. Corporations are increasingly concerned about the lives of their retirees. Whether this interest is manifested in preretirement counseling programs or in the extension of recreational programs and facilities, it marks a growing realization by business of the intensity of the relationship between worker and employer.

Companies such as Rainier Bank in Seattle, Wash.; Ameron and Security Pacific Bank in Los Angeles; Citibank, New York; and Pennsylvania Power and Light, Allentown, are among those that devote at least one session of preretirement counseling to getting people involved as volunteers after their retirement. At Cessna Aircraft in Wichita, Kan., the Retired Employees Association acts as a link between retirees and community groups for which they might wish to volunteer. Other companies, such as Equitable Life Assurance Society in New York, simply integrate retirees into ongoing employee volunteer programs. Recruitment is through company publications, special retiree luncheons, and word of mouth.

No matter how it happens, retired workers are becoming an important pool of talent for community agencies. Corporations can assist in mobilizing this pool, and in doing so, they can help make the elder years productive and rewarding for the retiree.

MONITORING THE PROGRAM

Although a few companies now do so, it is appropriate to measure the numbers of people who volunteer and the amount of service they offer. Clearly, a program that has well-developed goals, a detailed plan for how to achieve those goals, and some idea of how to measure success, will be more likely to address problems effectively. Without some organized method of monitoring volunteer activities, it is virtually impossible to assess their impact on the community, and there is no way that a corporation can adequately tell the story of its volunteers to the public.

One of the important benefits of volunteer programs to the company is that they enhance the company's image in the community. Few companies take adequate advantage of the possible public relations benefits to be gained by focusing public attention on the service activities on their employees.

3

Building a Successful Employee Volunteer Program

TWO factors are critical to a corporation's decision to undertake an employee volunteer program: sincere corporate interest and commitment of resources.

There must be a genuine interest on the part of the companies to assist the community. Often companies with programs only minimally encourage volunteers. They may have a released time policy, but it is poorly publicized. They may pay lip service to company involvement in a volunteer recruitment campaign, but they limit participation to a small segment of their workforce. They may be willing to assign staff to such a project, but they give the responsibility for planning and coordination to someone who is already overworked or who is not interested.

A company willing to encourage employee volunteers must also be willing to commit the necessary resources. Employee volunteer programs need not be expensive. But they are certainly not free. A corporation must be willing to invest at least in a part-time professional and provide the needed clerical support. Otherwise, it is better if the company does not attempt to launch a volunteer program in the first place.

CORPORATE COMMITMENT

There is no formula for successful employee volunteer programs. Much depends on the willingness of the company to make a clear commitment, and much more depends on the people chosen to design and implement the program. Each company is different and must find the kind of activity that is most comfortable for it. But with sincere commitment, adequate resources, and sound management, an employee volunteer program can meet the goal of serving the community, the company, and the employee.

The largest, most comprehensive, most enduring volunteer programs are those that are sponsored by companies where the chief executives take a personal interest in the programs, and devote some time to supporting and recognizing those employees who participate. The personal interest and commitment of the chief executive officer create the right atmosphere for encouraging employees to volunteer their services. In effect, the chief executive is saying to employees: "It is OK to volunteer. We think it is a legitimate activity and one that the company supports."

Volunteering must compete with a vast number of other activities. An almost insurmountable disadvantage arises if volunteering is not seen as a creditable activity with positive value within one's peer group. The corporation, therefore, must help to create this kind of an atmosphere.

People who volunteer are seeking to meet their own needs as well as to help others. Consequently, the extent to which they are comfortable in volunteering, in feeling that they are being satisfied, will help determine their willingness to continue participating. In the corporate setting, these needs are often complicated by the employee's concern that participation is not "approved", that it will in some way adversely affect his or her standing in the company.

Corporations can use the same marketing techniques they use with their customers to sell the volunteer program at every level of the company. The program must be seen as an extension of the company's concern for the total life of the employee, as a legitimate form of nonwork activity, as continuing education, as a recreation program, or as a hobby.

Employees must understand that their job status and security will be protected if they are given a leave of absence or time off. Middle managers and supervisors must be reassured that volunteering is an approved activity and a natural and realistic way to develop employees. Managers and supervisors must also understand the importance of volunteer work and the benefits that accrue from it to the company as well as to the community and to the employee.

PROVIDING RESOURCES

A natural link exists between a company's employee volunteer program and its corporate philanthrophy. Companies like Aetna (Dollars for Doers), Bank of America (Fund for Volunteer Service), Exxon (Community Service Fund), and Xerox (Community Involvement Program) have chosen to offer cash contributions to those agencies and organizations for which their employees volunteer.

Typically, such funds are available upon request by the employee. Usually earmarked for a specific project rather than for continuing operating expenses, the grants may be given to any tax-deductible, nonprofit organization. Employees making the request must be actively involved with the organization as volunteers, not just as members.

Grants may range from $500 to $5,000, and usually the company has some upper limit on the amount any single organization may receive in a given period of time. Some companies also match cash contributions made by employees to nonprofit organizations, similar to the contributions they make on a match basis to higher education.

A variation of this matching technique is practiced by McCormick and Company of Hunt Valley, Md. Its employees can contribute eight hours of overtime pay to their favorite charity, and the company will match the amount donated. The program, begun in 1941, encourages employees to work a "Charity Day" on Saturday, either donating the money earned through a payroll deduction, or donating eight hours of overtime.

In addition to these cash donations, companies make major contributions of goods and loaned facilities. When made available through an employee volunteer program, such contributions expand the resources available to community agencies and allow the company to monitor their use.

4

The Need
to Involve Industry

FROM all parts of the political spectrum has come the same cry: government can no longer—if it ever could—effectively meet the needs of all citizens. Indeed, there has been a growing public disillusionment with the ability of government to solve social problems generally.

Public positions taken by the two major presidential candidates in 1976 reflect these views:

> "One of the reasons our government has grown so large and unwieldy in recent years is that many of us have left the solution of our problems to the bureaucrats alone." *Jimmy Carter*

> "In recent years, government has proven time and again that it does not have all the answers for meeting our social needs. . . . Government and the private sector must join the search for new ways to utilize the flexibility, initiative, and expertise that characterize American problem-solving." *Gerald R. Ford*

The profit and nonprofit sectors have at least one thing in common: they are not the government. And although neither is necessarily anti-government, both have espoused a position of relative independence from the public sector. True, both have sought refuge in government regulation and government support when it was to their advantage to do so, but they also try to maintain their independence in order to retain their ability to pursue their own goals.

SOURCE OF TALENT

The fact is that corporations have the resources, both financial and human, needed to solve social problems.

The call for greater corporate involvement in solving social problems comes from government officials, community leaders, corporate critics, and business leaders themselves. Community organizations look to corporations for board members, contributions, and technical assistance. Public bodies from federal task forces on government reorganization to local taxing authorities regularly use loaned executives. Presumably such demands do not grow simply from a need for more bodies. Instead, they grow from a recognition that business is, in fact, quite good at what it does.

SOCIAL RESPONSIBILITY

In most communities, the corporation is the single most influential citizen. Its decisions have a far-reaching impact on the environment, the employment patterns, and the economy of the area, as well as on the daily lives of its own employees. By its very presence, it contributes to the growth, evolution, and vitality of the community. Increasingly, business leaders have recognized that such influence brings with it a responsibility.

As Stanley G. Karson, director of the Clearinghouse on Corporate Social Responsibility, puts it:

> "Corporate social responsibility is the commitment of the corporation conscious of its interdependence with the community to use its available resources in such a manner that they will impact positively on society."

But social responsibility is not a matter of altruism, but of self-interest. Mr. Karson himself said as much: "Corporate social responsibility, properly understood and exercised, is corporate self-interest."

In his introduction to *Participation II*, Atlantic Richfield's second audit of its corporate social responsibility activities, company president Thornton Bradshaw wrote:

> ". . . If this company chose to act as corporations once did— hewing close to business and disregarding larger obligations—its actions would be rejected because they did not look beyond the dollar sign to see the people."

During the social turmoil of the 1960s, many corporations discovered that their health was directly linked to the health of the communities in which they were located. Dying cities, stagnant local economies, disgruntled employees—these can all spell disaster for a profit-making company. Although some companies sought to escape such environments, others committed themselves to improving the life of their communities.

The Committee for Economic Development captured the essence of the matter when it stated: "People who have a good environment, education, and opportunity make better employees, customers, and neighbors for business than those who are poor, ignorant, and oppressed."

Appendix

IN 1977, the Board of Directors of the National Center for Voluntary Action (NCVA) initiated a new program, Volunteers from the Workplace, with the goal of assisting existing corporate volunteer programs and advocating the creation of new ones. This decision was a natural extension of NCVA's mission to stimulate and strengthen citizen involvement in problem-solving activities. With special funding assistance from the Charles Stewart Mott Foundation and the J.M. Foundation, NCVA undertook a comprehensive study of the nature and scope of corporate and union efforts to encourage and facilitate worker involvement in volunteering.

The study, completed early in 1979, had four specific outcomes. The first was the project's final report, *Volunteers from the Workplace*, a comprehensive, book-length examination of what corporations are doing and how they do it. The second was a national conference for those individuals in corporations and unions responsible for employee involvement programs. Held in Washington, D.C., in April 1979, the conference had over 150 participants, including representatives from 80 different companies.

The third outcome was increased public attention on corporate volunteer efforts. Finally, the project enabled NCVA to develop a continuing capability to provide information, training, and technical assistance services to those companies wishing to begin or expand an employee volunteer program. NCVA is the only national resource to which corporations can turn for a broad range of services in this area.

The Volunteers from the Workplace project focused primarily on the nation's largest corporations and only secondarily on the thousands of small, local businesses which actively contribute to the

30

community. The methodology of the study, while comprehensive, was relatively simple:

- A review of the available literature, both published and unpublished, including the files of such national, business-related organizations as the Clearinghouse on Corporate Social Responsibility of the American Council of Life Insurance, the Health Insurance Association of America, the Involvement Corps, and the Human Resources Network.
- A written survey of every Fortune 1000 company, of the 300 companies identified by Fortune as the largest in six nonindustrial areas, and of a random sample of 800 companies in each of three size categories from the 1978 Standard & Poor's Directory of Corporations.
- Telephone interviews, averaging 90 minutes each, with 135 companies and personal visits to 39 companies.
- A telephone survey of 50 companies for the purpose of learning more about the personal involvement of the chief executive officer in community volunteer activities.
- A written survey of Voluntary Action Centers (VACs) to determine whether and how they work with corporations. Follow-up phone interviews were conducted with 15 VACs.

A total of some 28 person-months were devoted to data collection and analysis.

A total of 364 companies responded to the various survey techniques, a yield of approximately 10 percent; 333 companies identified themselves as having some form of employee volunteer program. The data was analyzed to learn why such programs are created, how they are managed, and whether they are successful. Much of the information in the briefing is drawn from this research.